The Spirituality of Coziness Journal

Record 365 Days of Your Spiritual Experiences Through the Energy Of Coziness

MELISSA ALVAREZ

Published by

Adrema Press

Published by Adrema Press 2023

ISBN: 978-1-59611-146-2

Cover Design by Melissa Alvarez at https://BookCovers.us

OTHER BOOKS BY MELISSA ALVAREZ

365 Ways to Raise Your Frequency
365 Days to Raise Your Frequency Journal
Llewellyn's Little Book of Spirit Animals
Earth Frequency
Your Psychic Self
My Psychic Journal
Animal Frequency®
Animal Frequency® Journal
Animal Frequency® Oracle Cards
The Spirituality of Coziness
Believe and Receive
Believe and Receive Journal
Believe and Receive Mini Meditation Cards
Simply Give Thanks
Simply Give Thanks Gratitude Journal
Chakra Divination® Card & Charts Activity Book
Chakra Divination® Ultimate Balance Journal
The Essential Guide to Chakra Divination®
Chakra Divination® Card Deck
The Phoenix's Guide to Self-Renewal
Your Color Power
Analyze Your Handwriting
Ghosts, A Spirit Guide and A Past Life
Paranormal Investigative Groups Around the World

WRITING AS ARIANA DUPRE

Night Visions
Talgorian Prophecy
Talgorian Dragon
Briar Mountain
Paradise Designs
Paranormal Adventures

And much more...
Please Visit http://MelissaA.com for the complete booklist.

About the Author

Melissa Alvarez is a bestselling author, editor, and book cover designer who has written thirty-two books, novels, short stories, and mind/body/spirit nonfiction titles as well as nearly 500 articles on self-help, spirituality, and wellness. As a professional intuitive coach, energy worker, spiritual advisor, medium, and animal communicator with over 35 years of experience, Melissa has helped thousands of people bring clarity, joy, and balance into their lives. Melissa teaches others how to connect with their own intuitive nature and how to work with frequency for spiritual growth. She has appeared on number radio shows as both a guest and host. Melissa is the author of *365 Ways to Raise Your Frequency, Your Psychic Self, Animal Frequency, Earth Frequency, Llewellyn's Little Book of Spirit Animals, The Spirituality of Coziness, Simply Give Thanks* and many other titles. Her books with Llewellyn have been translated into multiple languages worldwide including Romanian, Russian, Chinese, French, Czech and Spanish. Please visit her website for a full list of her current titles.

Find Melissa Online at:
https://MelissaA.com
https://www.facebook.com/melissaalvarezauthor (main profile)
https://www.facebook.com/IamMelissaAlvarez (author page)

Other websites:
https://BookCovers.us
https://ThornRidge.com Online retail store
http://TopHatFriesians.com Barock Pinto & Friesian horses

The Spirituality of Coziness Journal is a companion to my book, *The Spirituality of Coziness: Experience Spiritual Growth through the Energy of Coziness for More Happiness, Contentment, and Satisfaction in Your Home, Relationships, and within Your Spiritual Self.* Please refer to the book and the detailed information that it contains as you journal. You can find *The Spirituality of Coziness* at all online retailers.

Date: ________________

Today I Connected with the Spirituality of Coziness by: _________

My Thoughts about the Experience: ___________________________

Date: ______________

Today I Connected with the Spirituality of Coziness by: ________

My Thoughts about the Experience: ____________________

Date: ________________

Today I Connected with the Spirituality of Coziness by: ________

My Thoughts about the Experience: ____________________

Date: ________________

Today I Connected with the Spirituality of Coziness by: _________

My Thoughts about the Experience: ________________________

Date: ________________

Today I Connected with the Spirituality of Coziness by: _________

My Thoughts about the Experience: ________________________

Date: ________________

Today I Connected with the Spirituality of Coziness by: ________

My Thoughts about the Experience: ________________________

Date: ______________

Today I Connected with the Spirituality of Coziness by: ________

My Thoughts about the Experience: ____________________

Date: ________________

Today I Connected with the Spirituality of Coziness by: _________

My Thoughts about the Experience: ________________________

Date: ______________

Today I Connected with the Spirituality of Coziness by: ________

My Thoughts about the Experience: ____________________

Date: ________________

Today I Connected with the Spirituality of Coziness by: ________

My Thoughts about the Experience: ________________________

Date: ______________

Today I Connected with the Spirituality of Coziness by: ________

My Thoughts about the Experience: ____________________

Date: ________________

Today I Connected with the Spirituality of Coziness by: _________

My Thoughts about the Experience: _________________________

Date: ________________

Today I Connected with the Spirituality of Coziness by: __________

My Thoughts about the Experience: ________________________

Date: ________________

Today I Connected with the Spirituality of Coziness by: _________

My Thoughts about the Experience: _________________________

Date: ________________

Today I Connected with the Spirituality of Coziness by: ________

My Thoughts about the Experience: ________________________

Date: ________________

Today I Connected with the Spirituality of Coziness by: ________

My Thoughts about the Experience: ________________________

Date: ______________

Today I Connected with the Spirituality of Coziness by: ________

My Thoughts about the Experience: ____________________

Date: ________________

Today I Connected with the Spirituality of Coziness by: ________

My Thoughts about the Experience: ________________________

Date: ________________

Today I Connected with the Spirituality of Coziness by: _________

My Thoughts about the Experience: __________________________

Date: ________________

Today I Connected with the Spirituality of Coziness by: ________

My Thoughts about the Experience: ________________________

Date: ________________

Today I Connected with the Spirituality of Coziness by: _________

My Thoughts about the Experience: ________________________

Date: ________________

Today I Connected with the Spirituality of Coziness by: _________

My Thoughts about the Experience: ___________________________

Date: ______________

Today I Connected with the Spirituality of Coziness by: ________

My Thoughts about the Experience: ____________________

Date: ________________

Today I Connected with the Spirituality of Coziness by: _________

My Thoughts about the Experience: ________________________

Date: ________________

Today I Connected with the Spirituality of Coziness by: _________

My Thoughts about the Experience: ___________________________

Date: ______________

Today I Connected with the Spirituality of Coziness by: ________

My Thoughts about the Experience: ______________________

Date: ________________

Today I Connected with the Spirituality of Coziness by: _________

My Thoughts about the Experience: ________________________

Date: ________________

Today I Connected with the Spirituality of Coziness by: ________

My Thoughts about the Experience: ________________________

Date: ________________

Today I Connected with the Spirituality of Coziness by: ________

My Thoughts about the Experience: ________________________

Date: ________________

Today I Connected with the Spirituality of Coziness by: _________

My Thoughts about the Experience: ________________________

Date: ________________

Today I Connected with the Spirituality of Coziness by: _________

My Thoughts about the Experience: ________________

Date: ________________

Today I Connected with the Spirituality of Coziness by: _________

My Thoughts about the Experience: _________________________

Date: ______________

Today I Connected with the Spirituality of Coziness by: ________

My Thoughts about the Experience: ______________________

Date: ________________

Today I Connected with the Spirituality of Coziness by: _________

My Thoughts about the Experience: ________________________

Date: ________________

Today I Connected with the Spirituality of Coziness by: ________

My Thoughts about the Experience: ________________________

Date: ________________

Today I Connected with the Spirituality of Coziness by: _________

My Thoughts about the Experience: ________________________

Date: ________________

Today I Connected with the Spirituality of Coziness by: ________

My Thoughts about the Experience: ________________________

Date: ________________

Today I Connected with the Spirituality of Coziness by: ________

My Thoughts about the Experience: ________________________

Date: ________________

Today I Connected with the Spirituality of Coziness by: ________

My Thoughts about the Experience: ________________________

Date: ________________

Today I Connected with the Spirituality of Coziness by: _________

My Thoughts about the Experience: _________________________

Date: ________________

Today I Connected with the Spirituality of Coziness by: _________

My Thoughts about the Experience: ________________________

Date: ________________

Today I Connected with the Spirituality of Coziness by: _________

My Thoughts about the Experience: ________________________

Date: ________________

Today I Connected with the Spirituality of Coziness by: ________

My Thoughts about the Experience: ________________________

Date: ________________

Today I Connected with the Spirituality of Coziness by: ________

My Thoughts about the Experience: ________________________

Date: ________________

Today I Connected with the Spirituality of Coziness by: ________

My Thoughts about the Experience: ________________________

Date: ________________

Today I Connected with the Spirituality of Coziness by: _________

My Thoughts about the Experience: ________________________

Date: ______________

Today I Connected with the Spirituality of Coziness by: ________

My Thoughts about the Experience: ____________________

Date: ________________

Today I Connected with the Spirituality of Coziness by: _________

My Thoughts about the Experience: ________________________

Date: ________________

Today I Connected with the Spirituality of Coziness by: ________

My Thoughts about the Experience: ________________________

Date: ________________

Today I Connected with the Spirituality of Coziness by: ________

My Thoughts about the Experience: ________________________

Date: ________________

Today I Connected with the Spirituality of Coziness by: ________

My Thoughts about the Experience: ________________________

Date: ______________

Today I Connected with the Spirituality of Coziness by: ________

My Thoughts about the Experience: ______________________

Date: ________________

Today I Connected with the Spirituality of Coziness by: _________

My Thoughts about the Experience: ________________________

Date: ________________

Today I Connected with the Spirituality of Coziness by: _________

My Thoughts about the Experience: _________________________

Date: ________________

Today I Connected with the Spirituality of Coziness by: ________

My Thoughts about the Experience: ________________________

Date: ________________

Today I Connected with the Spirituality of Coziness by: ________

My Thoughts about the Experience: ________________________

Date: ________________

Today I Connected with the Spirituality of Coziness by: _________

My Thoughts about the Experience: _________________________

Date: ________________

Today I Connected with the Spirituality of Coziness by: _________

My Thoughts about the Experience: _________________________

Date: ______________

Today I Connected with the Spirituality of Coziness by: ________

My Thoughts about the Experience: ____________________

Date: ________________

Today I Connected with the Spirituality of Coziness by: _________

My Thoughts about the Experience: ________________________

Date: ________________

Today I Connected with the Spirituality of Coziness by: ________

My Thoughts about the Experience: ________________________

Date: ________________

Today I Connected with the Spirituality of Coziness by: _________

My Thoughts about the Experience: ________________________

Date: ________________

Today I Connected with the Spirituality of Coziness by: ________

My Thoughts about the Experience: ________________________

Date: ________________

Today I Connected with the Spirituality of Coziness by: _________

My Thoughts about the Experience: ________________________

Date: ______________

Today I Connected with the Spirituality of Coziness by: ________

My Thoughts about the Experience: ____________________

Date: ________________

Today I Connected with the Spirituality of Coziness by: _________

My Thoughts about the Experience: ________________________

Date: ________________

Today I Connected with the Spirituality of Coziness by: _________

My Thoughts about the Experience: ________________________

Date: ________________

Today I Connected with the Spirituality of Coziness by: _________

My Thoughts about the Experience: ________________________

Date: ________________

Today I Connected with the Spirituality of Coziness by: _________

My Thoughts about the Experience: ________________________

Date: ________________

Today I Connected with the Spirituality of Coziness by: _________

My Thoughts about the Experience: ________________________

Date: ________________

Today I Connected with the Spirituality of Coziness by: ________

My Thoughts about the Experience: ____________________

Date: ________________

Today I Connected with the Spirituality of Coziness by: __________

My Thoughts about the Experience: ________________________

Date: ________________

Today I Connected with the Spirituality of Coziness by: ________

My Thoughts about the Experience: ________________________

Date: ________________

Today I Connected with the Spirituality of Coziness by: _________

My Thoughts about the Experience: ________________________

Date: ________________

Today I Connected with the Spirituality of Coziness by: _________

My Thoughts about the Experience: ___________________________

Date: ________________

Today I Connected with the Spirituality of Coziness by: _________

My Thoughts about the Experience: ________________________

Date: ________________

Today I Connected with the Spirituality of Coziness by: ________

My Thoughts about the Experience: ________________________

Date: ________________

Today I Connected with the Spirituality of Coziness by: _________

My Thoughts about the Experience: ________________________

Date: ______________

Today I Connected with the Spirituality of Coziness by: ________

My Thoughts about the Experience: ____________________

Date: ________________

Today I Connected with the Spirituality of Coziness by: _________

My Thoughts about the Experience: _________________________

Date: ______________

Today I Connected with the Spirituality of Coziness by: ________

My Thoughts about the Experience: ______________________

Date: ________________

Today I Connected with the Spirituality of Coziness by: _________

My Thoughts about the Experience: _________________________

Date: ________________

Today I Connected with the Spirituality of Coziness by: ________

My Thoughts about the Experience: ____________________

Date: ________________

Today I Connected with the Spirituality of Coziness by: ________

My Thoughts about the Experience: ________________________

Date: ______________

Today I Connected with the Spirituality of Coziness by: ________

My Thoughts about the Experience: ____________________

Date: ________________

Today I Connected with the Spirituality of Coziness by: ________

My Thoughts about the Experience: ________________________

Date: ________________

Today I Connected with the Spirituality of Coziness by: ________

My Thoughts about the Experience: ________________________

Date: ________________

Today I Connected with the Spirituality of Coziness by: _________

My Thoughts about the Experience: _________________________

Date: ________________

Today I Connected with the Spirituality of Coziness by: ________

My Thoughts about the Experience: ________________________

Date: ________________

Today I Connected with the Spirituality of Coziness by: _________

My Thoughts about the Experience: ________________________

Date: ______________

Today I Connected with the Spirituality of Coziness by: ________

My Thoughts about the Experience: ______________________

Date: ________________

Today I Connected with the Spirituality of Coziness by: _________

My Thoughts about the Experience: _________________________

Date: ______________

Today I Connected with the Spirituality of Coziness by: ________

My Thoughts about the Experience: ____________________

Date: ________________

Today I Connected with the Spirituality of Coziness by: ________

My Thoughts about the Experience: ________________________

Date: ________________

Today I Connected with the Spirituality of Coziness by: _________

My Thoughts about the Experience: ________________________

Date: ________________

Today I Connected with the Spirituality of Coziness by: _________

My Thoughts about the Experience: __________________________

Date: ______________

Today I Connected with the Spirituality of Coziness by: ________

My Thoughts about the Experience: ____________________

Date: ________________

Today I Connected with the Spirituality of Coziness by: _________

My Thoughts about the Experience: _________________________

Date: ________________

Today I Connected with the Spirituality of Coziness by: _________

My Thoughts about the Experience: ________________________

Date: ______________

Today I Connected with the Spirituality of Coziness by: ________

My Thoughts about the Experience: ______________________

Date: ______________

Today I Connected with the Spirituality of Coziness by: ________

My Thoughts about the Experience: ____________________

Date: ________________

Today I Connected with the Spirituality of Coziness by: ________

My Thoughts about the Experience: ________________________

Date: ________________

Today I Connected with the Spirituality of Coziness by: ________

My Thoughts about the Experience: ________________________

Date: ________________

Today I Connected with the Spirituality of Coziness by: _________

My Thoughts about the Experience: _________________________

Date: ________________

Today I Connected with the Spirituality of Coziness by: ________

My Thoughts about the Experience: ________________________

Date: ________________

Today I Connected with the Spirituality of Coziness by: _________

My Thoughts about the Experience: _________________________

Date: ________________

Today I Connected with the Spirituality of Coziness by: ________

My Thoughts about the Experience: ________________________

Date: ________________

Today I Connected with the Spirituality of Coziness by: _________

My Thoughts about the Experience: _________________________

Date: ________________

Today I Connected with the Spirituality of Coziness by: ________

My Thoughts about the Experience: ________________________

Date: ________________

Today I Connected with the Spirituality of Coziness by: _________

My Thoughts about the Experience: __________________________

Date: ______________

Today I Connected with the Spirituality of Coziness by: ________

My Thoughts about the Experience: ______________________

Date: ________________

Today I Connected with the Spirituality of Coziness by: _________

My Thoughts about the Experience: ________________________

Date: ______________

Today I Connected with the Spirituality of Coziness by: ________

My Thoughts about the Experience: ____________________

Date: ________________

Today I Connected with the Spirituality of Coziness by: _________

My Thoughts about the Experience: ________________________

Date: ________________

Today I Connected with the Spirituality of Coziness by: _________

My Thoughts about the Experience: ________________________

Date: ________________

Today I Connected with the Spirituality of Coziness by: _________

My Thoughts about the Experience: _________________________

Date: ______________

Today I Connected with the Spirituality of Coziness by: ________

My Thoughts about the Experience: ______________________

Date: ______________

Today I Connected with the Spirituality of Coziness by: ________

My Thoughts about the Experience: ______________________

Date: ________________

Today I Connected with the Spirituality of Coziness by: _________

My Thoughts about the Experience: _________________________

Date: ________________

Today I Connected with the Spirituality of Coziness by: _________

My Thoughts about the Experience: __________________________

Date: ________________

Today I Connected with the Spirituality of Coziness by: _________

My Thoughts about the Experience: ____________________

Date: ________________

Today I Connected with the Spirituality of Coziness by: _________

My Thoughts about the Experience: ________________________

Date: ______________

Today I Connected with the Spirituality of Coziness by: ________

My Thoughts about the Experience: ____________________

Date: ________________

Today I Connected with the Spirituality of Coziness by: ________

My Thoughts about the Experience: ________________________

Date: ________________

Today I Connected with the Spirituality of Coziness by: ________

My Thoughts about the Experience: ________________________

Date: ________________

Today I Connected with the Spirituality of Coziness by: _________

My Thoughts about the Experience: ___________________________

Date: ________________

Today I Connected with the Spirituality of Coziness by: ________

My Thoughts about the Experience: ________________________

Date: ________________

Today I Connected with the Spirituality of Coziness by: _________

My Thoughts about the Experience: ________________________

Date: ________________

Today I Connected with the Spirituality of Coziness by: _________

My Thoughts about the Experience: ________________________

Date: ________________

Today I Connected with the Spirituality of Coziness by: _________

My Thoughts about the Experience: ________________________

Date: ________________

Today I Connected with the Spirituality of Coziness by: __________

My Thoughts about the Experience: ____________________

Date: ________________

Today I Connected with the Spirituality of Coziness by: _________

My Thoughts about the Experience: _________________________

Date: ________________

Today I Connected with the Spirituality of Coziness by: ________

My Thoughts about the Experience: ________________________

Date: ________________

Today I Connected with the Spirituality of Coziness by: _________

My Thoughts about the Experience: _________________________

Date: ________________

Today I Connected with the Spirituality of Coziness by: _________

My Thoughts about the Experience: ________________________

Date: ________________

Today I Connected with the Spirituality of Coziness by: _________

My Thoughts about the Experience: ________________________

Date: ________________

Today I Connected with the Spirituality of Coziness by: _________

My Thoughts about the Experience: ________________________

Date: ________________

Today I Connected with the Spirituality of Coziness by: _________

My Thoughts about the Experience: ________________________

Date: ______________

Today I Connected with the Spirituality of Coziness by: ________

My Thoughts about the Experience: ______________________

Date: ________________

Today I Connected with the Spirituality of Coziness by: _________

My Thoughts about the Experience: ______________________

Date: ________________

Today I Connected with the Spirituality of Coziness by: __________

My Thoughts about the Experience: ____________________

Date: ________________

Today I Connected with the Spirituality of Coziness by: _________

My Thoughts about the Experience: _________________________

Date: ____________

Today I Connected with the Spirituality of Coziness by: ________

My Thoughts about the Experience: ____________________

Date: ________________

Today I Connected with the Spirituality of Coziness by: _________

My Thoughts about the Experience: __________________________

Date: ________________

Today I Connected with the Spirituality of Coziness by: ________

My Thoughts about the Experience: ________________________

Date: ________________

Today I Connected with the Spirituality of Coziness by: _________

My Thoughts about the Experience: _________________________

Date: ________________

Today I Connected with the Spirituality of Coziness by: _________

My Thoughts about the Experience: ________________________

Date: ________________

Today I Connected with the Spirituality of Coziness by: ________

My Thoughts about the Experience: ________________________

Date: ________________

Today I Connected with the Spirituality of Coziness by: _________

My Thoughts about the Experience: ________________________

Date: ________________

Today I Connected with the Spirituality of Coziness by: _________

My Thoughts about the Experience: ________________________

Date: ________________

Today I Connected with the Spirituality of Coziness by: ________

My Thoughts about the Experience: ____________________

Date: ________________

Today I Connected with the Spirituality of Coziness by: ________

My Thoughts about the Experience: ______________________

Date: ________________

Today I Connected with the Spirituality of Coziness by: ________

My Thoughts about the Experience: ________________________

Date: ________________

Today I Connected with the Spirituality of Coziness by: _________

My Thoughts about the Experience: ________________________

Date: _______________

Today I Connected with the Spirituality of Coziness by: ________

My Thoughts about the Experience: ____________________

Date: ______________

Today I Connected with the Spirituality of Coziness by: ________

My Thoughts about the Experience: ______________________

Date: ______________

Today I Connected with the Spirituality of Coziness by: ________

My Thoughts about the Experience: ______________________

Date: ________________

Today I Connected with the Spirituality of Coziness by: _________

My Thoughts about the Experience: ________________________

Date: ________________

Today I Connected with the Spirituality of Coziness by: _________

My Thoughts about the Experience: ________________________

Date: ________________

Today I Connected with the Spirituality of Coziness by: _________

My Thoughts about the Experience: __________________________

Date: ________________

Today I Connected with the Spirituality of Coziness by: _________

My Thoughts about the Experience: ________________________

Date: ________________

Today I Connected with the Spirituality of Coziness by: _________

My Thoughts about the Experience: ______________________

Date: ________________

Today I Connected with the Spirituality of Coziness by: ________

My Thoughts about the Experience: ________________________

Date: ________________

Today I Connected with the Spirituality of Coziness by: _________

My Thoughts about the Experience: ________________________

Date: ________________

Today I Connected with the Spirituality of Coziness by: _________

My Thoughts about the Experience: ________________________

Date: ________________

Today I Connected with the Spirituality of Coziness by: ________

My Thoughts about the Experience: ________________________

Date: ________________

Today I Connected with the Spirituality of Coziness by: _________

My Thoughts about the Experience: ________________________

Date: ________________

Today I Connected with the Spirituality of Coziness by: ________

My Thoughts about the Experience: ________________________

Date: ________________

Today I Connected with the Spirituality of Coziness by: _________

My Thoughts about the Experience: ________________________

Date: ________________

Today I Connected with the Spirituality of Coziness by: _________

My Thoughts about the Experience: _________________________

Date: ______________

Today I Connected with the Spirituality of Coziness by: ________

My Thoughts about the Experience: ____________________

Date: ________________

Today I Connected with the Spirituality of Coziness by: _________

My Thoughts about the Experience: _________________________

Date: ______________

Today I Connected with the Spirituality of Coziness by: ________

My Thoughts about the Experience: ______________________

Date: ________________

Today I Connected with the Spirituality of Coziness by: _________

My Thoughts about the Experience: ________________________

Date: ________________

Today I Connected with the Spirituality of Coziness by: ________

My Thoughts about the Experience: ________________________

Date: ________________

Today I Connected with the Spirituality of Coziness by: ________

My Thoughts about the Experience: ________________________

Date: ________________

Today I Connected with the Spirituality of Coziness by: ________

My Thoughts about the Experience: ________________________

Date: ________________

Today I Connected with the Spirituality of Coziness by: _________

My Thoughts about the Experience: ________________________

Date: ________________

Today I Connected with the Spirituality of Coziness by: _________

My Thoughts about the Experience: ________________________

Date: ________________

Today I Connected with the Spirituality of Coziness by: ________

My Thoughts about the Experience: ________________________

Date: ________________

Today I Connected with the Spirituality of Coziness by: ________

My Thoughts about the Experience: ________________________

Date: ________________

Today I Connected with the Spirituality of Coziness by: ________

My Thoughts about the Experience: ________________________

Date: ________________

Today I Connected with the Spirituality of Coziness by: _________

My Thoughts about the Experience: ________________________

Date: ________________

Today I Connected with the Spirituality of Coziness by: _________

My Thoughts about the Experience: __________________________

Date: ________________

Today I Connected with the Spirituality of Coziness by: _________

My Thoughts about the Experience: _________________________

Date: ________________

Today I Connected with the Spirituality of Coziness by: _________

My Thoughts about the Experience: __________________________

Date: ________________

Today I Connected with the Spirituality of Coziness by: _________

My Thoughts about the Experience: ________________________

Date: ________________

Today I Connected with the Spirituality of Coziness by: _________

My Thoughts about the Experience: _________________________

Date: ________________

Today I Connected with the Spirituality of Coziness by: _________

My Thoughts about the Experience: ________________________

Date: ________________

Today I Connected with the Spirituality of Coziness by: _________

My Thoughts about the Experience: _________________________

Date: ______________

Today I Connected with the Spirituality of Coziness by: ________

My Thoughts about the Experience: ____________________

Date: ________________

Today I Connected with the Spirituality of Coziness by: _________

My Thoughts about the Experience: ________________________

Date: ________________

Today I Connected with the Spirituality of Coziness by: ________

My Thoughts about the Experience: ________________________

Date: ________________

Today I Connected with the Spirituality of Coziness by: _________

My Thoughts about the Experience: _________________________

Date: ________________

Today I Connected with the Spirituality of Coziness by: ________

My Thoughts about the Experience: ________________________

Date: ________________

Today I Connected with the Spirituality of Coziness by: _________

My Thoughts about the Experience: __________________________

Date: ________________

Today I Connected with the Spirituality of Coziness by: ________

My Thoughts about the Experience: ________________________

Date: _______________

Today I Connected with the Spirituality of Coziness by: ________

My Thoughts about the Experience: ______________________

Date: _______________

Today I Connected with the Spirituality of Coziness by: ________

My Thoughts about the Experience: ________________________

Date: ________________

Today I Connected with the Spirituality of Coziness by: _________

My Thoughts about the Experience: ________________________

Date: ________________

Today I Connected with the Spirituality of Coziness by: _________

My Thoughts about the Experience: ________________________

Date: ________________

Today I Connected with the Spirituality of Coziness by: ________

My Thoughts about the Experience: ________________________

Date: ________________

Today I Connected with the Spirituality of Coziness by: _________

My Thoughts about the Experience: ________________________

Date: ______________

Today I Connected with the Spirituality of Coziness by: ________

My Thoughts about the Experience: ____________________

Date: ______________

Today I Connected with the Spirituality of Coziness by: ________

My Thoughts about the Experience: ______________________

Date: ________________

Today I Connected with the Spirituality of Coziness by: ________

My Thoughts about the Experience: ________________________

Date: ________________

Today I Connected with the Spirituality of Coziness by: ________

My Thoughts about the Experience: ________________________

Date: ________________

Today I Connected with the Spirituality of Coziness by: _________

My Thoughts about the Experience: ________________________

Date: ________________

Today I Connected with the Spirituality of Coziness by: ________

My Thoughts about the Experience: ________________________

Date: ________________

Today I Connected with the Spirituality of Coziness by: _________

My Thoughts about the Experience: _________________________

Date: ________________

Today I Connected with the Spirituality of Coziness by: ________

My Thoughts about the Experience: ______________________

Date: ________________

Today I Connected with the Spirituality of Coziness by: _________

My Thoughts about the Experience: ________________________

Date: ________________

Today I Connected with the Spirituality of Coziness by: ________

My Thoughts about the Experience: ________________________

Date: ________________

Today I Connected with the Spirituality of Coziness by: _________

My Thoughts about the Experience: _________________________

Date: ________________

Today I Connected with the Spirituality of Coziness by: _________

My Thoughts about the Experience: ________________________

Date: ________________

Today I Connected with the Spirituality of Coziness by: _________

My Thoughts about the Experience: _________________________

Date: ______________

Today I Connected with the Spirituality of Coziness by: ________

My Thoughts about the Experience: ______________________

Date: ________________

Today I Connected with the Spirituality of Coziness by: _________

My Thoughts about the Experience: _________________________

Date: ________________

Today I Connected with the Spirituality of Coziness by: _________

My Thoughts about the Experience: ____________________

Date: ________________

Today I Connected with the Spirituality of Coziness by: ________

My Thoughts about the Experience: ________________________

Date: ________________

Today I Connected with the Spirituality of Coziness by: _________

My Thoughts about the Experience: ____________________

Date: ________________

Today I Connected with the Spirituality of Coziness by: ________

My Thoughts about the Experience: ________________________

Date: ________________

Today I Connected with the Spirituality of Coziness by: ________

My Thoughts about the Experience: ________________________

Date: ________________

Today I Connected with the Spirituality of Coziness by: _________

My Thoughts about the Experience: __________________________

Date: ________________

Today I Connected with the Spirituality of Coziness by: _________

My Thoughts about the Experience: ________________________

Date: ________________

Today I Connected with the Spirituality of Coziness by: _________

My Thoughts about the Experience: __________________________

Date: ________________

Today I Connected with the Spirituality of Coziness by: _________

My Thoughts about the Experience: ________________________

Date: ________________

Today I Connected with the Spirituality of Coziness by: _________

My Thoughts about the Experience: ________________________

Date: ________________

Today I Connected with the Spirituality of Coziness by: ________

My Thoughts about the Experience: ________________________

Date: ________________

Today I Connected with the Spirituality of Coziness by: ________

My Thoughts about the Experience: ________________________

Date: ________________

Today I Connected with the Spirituality of Coziness by: _________

My Thoughts about the Experience: _________________________

Date: ________________

Today I Connected with the Spirituality of Coziness by: _________

My Thoughts about the Experience: ________________________

Date: ______________

Today I Connected with the Spirituality of Coziness by: ________

My Thoughts about the Experience: ____________________

Date: ________________

Today I Connected with the Spirituality of Coziness by: _________

My Thoughts about the Experience: __________________________

Date: ______________

Today I Connected with the Spirituality of Coziness by: ________

My Thoughts about the Experience: ______________________

Date: ________________

Today I Connected with the Spirituality of Coziness by: ________

My Thoughts about the Experience: ________________________

Date: ______________

Today I Connected with the Spirituality of Coziness by: ________

My Thoughts about the Experience: ______________________

Date: ________________

Today I Connected with the Spirituality of Coziness by: _________

My Thoughts about the Experience: ___________________________

Date: ________________

Today I Connected with the Spirituality of Coziness by: _________

My Thoughts about the Experience: _________________________

Date: ______________

Today I Connected with the Spirituality of Coziness by: ________

My Thoughts about the Experience: ______________________

Date: ________________

Today I Connected with the Spirituality of Coziness by: ________

My Thoughts about the Experience: ________________________

Date: ________________

Today I Connected with the Spirituality of Coziness by: _________

My Thoughts about the Experience: _________________________

Date: ________________

Today I Connected with the Spirituality of Coziness by: _________

My Thoughts about the Experience: ________________________

Date: ________________

Today I Connected with the Spirituality of Coziness by: _________

My Thoughts about the Experience: _________________________

Date: ________________

Today I Connected with the Spirituality of Coziness by: _________

My Thoughts about the Experience: ________________________

Date: ________________

Today I Connected with the Spirituality of Coziness by: _________

My Thoughts about the Experience: _________________________

Date: ________________

Today I Connected with the Spirituality of Coziness by: ________

My Thoughts about the Experience: ________________________

Date: ________________

Today I Connected with the Spirituality of Coziness by: _________

My Thoughts about the Experience: _________________________

Date: ________________

Today I Connected with the Spirituality of Coziness by: _________

My Thoughts about the Experience: ________________________

Date: ________________

Today I Connected with the Spirituality of Coziness by: _________

My Thoughts about the Experience: ________________________

Date: ________________

Today I Connected with the Spirituality of Coziness by: _________

My Thoughts about the Experience: ________________________

Date: ______________

Today I Connected with the Spirituality of Coziness by: ________

My Thoughts about the Experience: ______________________

Date: ________________

Today I Connected with the Spirituality of Coziness by: ________

My Thoughts about the Experience: ________________________

Date: ________________

Today I Connected with the Spirituality of Coziness by: ________

My Thoughts about the Experience: ________________________

Date: ________________

Today I Connected with the Spirituality of Coziness by: ________

My Thoughts about the Experience: ________________________

Date: ________________

Today I Connected with the Spirituality of Coziness by: ________

My Thoughts about the Experience: ________________________

Date: ________________

Today I Connected with the Spirituality of Coziness by: _________

My Thoughts about the Experience: ________________________

Date: ________________

Today I Connected with the Spirituality of Coziness by: _________

My Thoughts about the Experience: __________________________

Date: ________________

Today I Connected with the Spirituality of Coziness by: ________

My Thoughts about the Experience: ________________________

Date: ________________

Today I Connected with the Spirituality of Coziness by: ________

My Thoughts about the Experience: ________________________

Date: ________________

Today I Connected with the Spirituality of Coziness by: _________

My Thoughts about the Experience: ________________________

Date: ________________

Today I Connected with the Spirituality of Coziness by: _________

My Thoughts about the Experience: _________________________

Date: ________________

Today I Connected with the Spirituality of Coziness by: _________

My Thoughts about the Experience: ________________________

Date: ________________

Today I Connected with the Spirituality of Coziness by: ________

My Thoughts about the Experience: ________________________

Date: ________________

Today I Connected with the Spirituality of Coziness by: ________

My Thoughts about the Experience: ________________________

Date: ________________

Today I Connected with the Spirituality of Coziness by: _________

My Thoughts about the Experience: ________________________

Date: ________________

Today I Connected with the Spirituality of Coziness by: _________

My Thoughts about the Experience: ________________________

Date: ________________

Today I Connected with the Spirituality of Coziness by: _________

My Thoughts about the Experience: _________________________

Date: ________________

Today I Connected with the Spirituality of Coziness by: ________

My Thoughts about the Experience: ________________________

Date: ________________

Today I Connected with the Spirituality of Coziness by: ________

My Thoughts about the Experience: ________________________

Date: ______________

Today I Connected with the Spirituality of Coziness by: ________

My Thoughts about the Experience: ____________________

Date: ________________

Today I Connected with the Spirituality of Coziness by: _________

My Thoughts about the Experience: _________________________

Date: ________________

Today I Connected with the Spirituality of Coziness by: _________

My Thoughts about the Experience: _________________________

Date: ________________

Today I Connected with the Spirituality of Coziness by: ________

My Thoughts about the Experience: ________________________

Date: ________________

Today I Connected with the Spirituality of Coziness by: _________

My Thoughts about the Experience: ____________________

Date: ________________

Today I Connected with the Spirituality of Coziness by: _________

My Thoughts about the Experience: ________________________

Date: ________________

Today I Connected with the Spirituality of Coziness by: ________

My Thoughts about the Experience: ________________________

Date: ________________

Today I Connected with the Spirituality of Coziness by: _________

My Thoughts about the Experience: ________________________

Date: ________________

Today I Connected with the Spirituality of Coziness by: ________

My Thoughts about the Experience: ________________________

Date: ________________

Today I Connected with the Spirituality of Coziness by: _________

My Thoughts about the Experience: _________________________

Date: ________________

Today I Connected with the Spirituality of Coziness by: _________

My Thoughts about the Experience: ________________________

Date: ________________

Today I Connected with the Spirituality of Coziness by: _________

My Thoughts about the Experience: ________________________

Date: ______________

Today I Connected with the Spirituality of Coziness by: ________

My Thoughts about the Experience: ____________________

Date: ________________

Today I Connected with the Spirituality of Coziness by: _________

My Thoughts about the Experience: _________________________

Date: ________________

Today I Connected with the Spirituality of Coziness by: _________

My Thoughts about the Experience: ________________________

Date: ________________

Today I Connected with the Spirituality of Coziness by: ________

My Thoughts about the Experience: ________________________

Date: ________________

Today I Connected with the Spirituality of Coziness by: __________

My Thoughts about the Experience: ____________________

Date: ________________

Today I Connected with the Spirituality of Coziness by: _________

My Thoughts about the Experience: _________________________

Date: ________________

Today I Connected with the Spirituality of Coziness by: ________

My Thoughts about the Experience: ________________________

Date: ________________

Today I Connected with the Spirituality of Coziness by: _________

My Thoughts about the Experience: _________________________

Date: ________________

Today I Connected with the Spirituality of Coziness by: ________

My Thoughts about the Experience: ________________________

Date: ________________

Today I Connected with the Spirituality of Coziness by: __________

My Thoughts about the Experience: ________________________

Date: ________________

Today I Connected with the Spirituality of Coziness by: _________

My Thoughts about the Experience: ________________________

Date: ________________

Today I Connected with the Spirituality of Coziness by: _________

My Thoughts about the Experience: ______________________

Date: ________________

Today I Connected with the Spirituality of Coziness by: _________

My Thoughts about the Experience: ________________________

Date: ________________

Today I Connected with the Spirituality of Coziness by: _________

My Thoughts about the Experience: ________________________

Date: ________________

Today I Connected with the Spirituality of Coziness by: _________

My Thoughts about the Experience: ________________________

Date: ________________

Today I Connected with the Spirituality of Coziness by: _________

My Thoughts about the Experience: ________________________

Date: ________________

Today I Connected with the Spirituality of Coziness by: _________

My Thoughts about the Experience: ________________________

Date: ________________

Today I Connected with the Spirituality of Coziness by: _________

My Thoughts about the Experience: ____________________________

Date: ______________

Today I Connected with the Spirituality of Coziness by: ________

My Thoughts about the Experience: ______________________

Date: ________________

Today I Connected with the Spirituality of Coziness by: _________

My Thoughts about the Experience: ________________________

Date: ________________

Today I Connected with the Spirituality of Coziness by: _________

My Thoughts about the Experience: ________________________

Date: ________________

Today I Connected with the Spirituality of Coziness by: ________

My Thoughts about the Experience: ________________________

Date: ________________

Today I Connected with the Spirituality of Coziness by: ________

My Thoughts about the Experience: ________________________

Date: ________________

Today I Connected with the Spirituality of Coziness by: _________

My Thoughts about the Experience: ________________________

Date: ________________

Today I Connected with the Spirituality of Coziness by: ________

My Thoughts about the Experience: ________________________

Date: ________________

Today I Connected with the Spirituality of Coziness by: ________

My Thoughts about the Experience: ________________________

Date: ______________

Today I Connected with the Spirituality of Coziness by: ________

My Thoughts about the Experience: ______________________

Date: ________________

Today I Connected with the Spirituality of Coziness by: _________

My Thoughts about the Experience: ________________________

Date: ________________

Today I Connected with the Spirituality of Coziness by: ________

My Thoughts about the Experience: ________________________

Date: ________________

Today I Connected with the Spirituality of Coziness by: _________

My Thoughts about the Experience: ________________________

Date: ______________

Today I Connected with the Spirituality of Coziness by: ________

My Thoughts about the Experience: ______________________

Date: ________________

Today I Connected with the Spirituality of Coziness by: _________

My Thoughts about the Experience: ________________________

Date: ________________

Today I Connected with the Spirituality of Coziness by: ________

My Thoughts about the Experience: ________________________

Date: ________________

Today I Connected with the Spirituality of Coziness by: _________

My Thoughts about the Experience: ________________________

Date: ________________

Today I Connected with the Spirituality of Coziness by: ________

My Thoughts about the Experience: ________________________

Date: ________________

Today I Connected with the Spirituality of Coziness by: ________

My Thoughts about the Experience: ________________________

Date: ________________

Today I Connected with the Spirituality of Coziness by: ________

My Thoughts about the Experience: ____________________

Date: ________________

Today I Connected with the Spirituality of Coziness by: _________

My Thoughts about the Experience: ________________________

Date: ________________

Today I Connected with the Spirituality of Coziness by: _________

My Thoughts about the Experience: ________________________

Date: ________________

Today I Connected with the Spirituality of Coziness by: _________

My Thoughts about the Experience: ________________________

Date: ________________

Today I Connected with the Spirituality of Coziness by: ________

My Thoughts about the Experience: ________________________

Date: ________________

Today I Connected with the Spirituality of Coziness by: _________

My Thoughts about the Experience: _________________________

Date: ______________

Today I Connected with the Spirituality of Coziness by: ________

My Thoughts about the Experience: ____________________

Date: ________________

Today I Connected with the Spirituality of Coziness by: _________

My Thoughts about the Experience: ______________________

Date: ________________

Today I Connected with the Spirituality of Coziness by: _________

My Thoughts about the Experience: _______________________

Date: ________________

Today I Connected with the Spirituality of Coziness by: ________

My Thoughts about the Experience: ________________________

Date: ________________

Today I Connected with the Spirituality of Coziness by: _________

My Thoughts about the Experience: ________________________

Date: ________________

Today I Connected with the Spirituality of Coziness by: ________

My Thoughts about the Experience: ________________________

Date: ________________

Today I Connected with the Spirituality of Coziness by: _________

My Thoughts about the Experience: ________________________

Date: ________________

Today I Connected with the Spirituality of Coziness by: ________

My Thoughts about the Experience: ________________________

Date: ________________

Today I Connected with the Spirituality of Coziness by: ________

My Thoughts about the Experience: ________________________

Date: ________________

Today I Connected with the Spirituality of Coziness by: _________

My Thoughts about the Experience: __________________________

Date: ________________

Today I Connected with the Spirituality of Coziness by: ________

My Thoughts about the Experience: ________________________

Date: ________________

Today I Connected with the Spirituality of Coziness by: _________

My Thoughts about the Experience: ________________________

Date: ________________

Today I Connected with the Spirituality of Coziness by: ________

My Thoughts about the Experience: ________________________

Date: ________________

Today I Connected with the Spirituality of Coziness by: _________

My Thoughts about the Experience: _________________________

Date: ________________

Today I Connected with the Spirituality of Coziness by: ________

My Thoughts about the Experience: ________________________

Date: ______________

Today I Connected with the Spirituality of Coziness by: ________

My Thoughts about the Experience: ____________________

Date: ________________

Today I Connected with the Spirituality of Coziness by: _________

My Thoughts about the Experience: ________________________

Date: ________________

Today I Connected with the Spirituality of Coziness by: _________

My Thoughts about the Experience: ______________________

Date: ______________

Today I Connected with the Spirituality of Coziness by: ________

My Thoughts about the Experience: ____________________

Date: ________________

Today I Connected with the Spirituality of Coziness by: _________

My Thoughts about the Experience: __________________________

Date: ______________

Today I Connected with the Spirituality of Coziness by: ________

My Thoughts about the Experience: ____________________

Date: ________________

Today I Connected with the Spirituality of Coziness by: _________

My Thoughts about the Experience: _________________________

Date: ________________

Today I Connected with the Spirituality of Coziness by: _________

My Thoughts about the Experience: ________________________

Date: ________________

Today I Connected with the Spirituality of Coziness by: _________

My Thoughts about the Experience: __________________________

Date: ________________

Today I Connected with the Spirituality of Coziness by: ________

My Thoughts about the Experience: ________________________

Date: ________________

Today I Connected with the Spirituality of Coziness by: _________

My Thoughts about the Experience: ________________________

Date: ________________

Today I Connected with the Spirituality of Coziness by: ________

My Thoughts about the Experience: ________________________

Date: ________________

Today I Connected with the Spirituality of Coziness by: _________

My Thoughts about the Experience: __________________________

Date: ________________

Today I Connected with the Spirituality of Coziness by: _________

My Thoughts about the Experience: _________________________

Date: ________________

Today I Connected with the Spirituality of Coziness by: __________

My Thoughts about the Experience: __________________________

Date: ________________

Today I Connected with the Spirituality of Coziness by: ________

My Thoughts about the Experience: ________________________

Date: ________________

Today I Connected with the Spirituality of Coziness by: ________

My Thoughts about the Experience: ________________________

Date: _______________

Today I Connected with the Spirituality of Coziness by: ________

My Thoughts about the Experience: ________________________

Date: _______________

Today I Connected with the Spirituality of Coziness by: _________

My Thoughts about the Experience: ________________________

Date: ________________

Today I Connected with the Spirituality of Coziness by: ________

My Thoughts about the Experience: ________________________

Date: ________________

Today I Connected with the Spirituality of Coziness by: _________

My Thoughts about the Experience: _________________________

Date: ______________

Today I Connected with the Spirituality of Coziness by: ________

My Thoughts about the Experience: ______________________

Date: ______________

Today I Connected with the Spirituality of Coziness by: ________

My Thoughts about the Experience: ____________________

Date: ________________

Today I Connected with the Spirituality of Coziness by: ________

My Thoughts about the Experience: ________________________

Date: ________________

Today I Connected with the Spirituality of Coziness by: ________

My Thoughts about the Experience: ____________________

Date: ________________

Today I Connected with the Spirituality of Coziness by: __________

My Thoughts about the Experience: ____________________

Congratulations! You've now connected with the Spirituality of Coziness for an entire year!

VISIT MELISSA ALVAREZ ONLINE AT
www.MelissaA.com
Email Melissa at media@melissaa.com

www.ingramcontent.com/pod-product-compliance
Lightning Source LLC
Chambersburg PA
CBHW052342090426
42740CB00040B/2522
* 9 7 8 1 5 9 6 1 1 1 4 6 2 *